A scene from the Bloomsburg Theatre Ensemble production of *The Women of Lockerbie*, in Bloomsburg, Pennsylvania.

THE WOMEN
OF LOCKERBIE

BY DEBORAH BREVOORT

★

★

DRAMATISTS
PLAY SERVICE
INC.

THE WOMEN OF LOCKERBIE
Copyright © 2005, Deborah Brevoort

All Rights Reserved

AUTHOR'S NOTE

When I began work on *The Women of Lockerbie*, I set out to write the play in the form of the Greek tragedy. There was something about the scale of the horror that was unleashed on Lockerbie, Scotland, the size of the emotions experienced by the victim's families and the heroic scope of the laundry project that said "Greek" to me. After all, the form of the Greek tragedy was designed to tell these kinds of stories, the horrible stories like Lockerbie, of holocausts, wars, plagues, and genocide. It was a form designed to handle the big emotions and extreme behaviors that attend these kinds of events by presenting them in a way that the audience can bear.

During the writing of the play, my original hunch proved to be right. Naturalism as a theatrical form was simply inadequate in capturing the dimensions of this story and whenever the play veered in that direction, the characters and situation sunk to the level of melodrama. I found that the trick to keeping the play heightened was to stick closely to the conventions used by the Greeks. The episode/dialogue/ode structure as well as the use of theatrical conventions such as stichomythia, poetic speech, recited language and heightened gestures showed me how to calibrate emotion, thought, engagement and distancing effects within the performance so that the audience can not only endure the spectacle on stage, but enjoy it and experience catharsis. I also realized how specific the form was — every element was precisely arranged with a mind to what the audience can, and cannot take, at any given moment. In other words, the structure had "rhythm."

Writing *The Women of Lockerbie* taught me to trust the form, even when I didn't always understand it. In the end, it was the form, as opposed to the characters or situations, that led me to the conclusion of the play and revealed to me moment by moment how the story had to be told.

My advice to the actors and directors of *The Women of Lockerbie* is to trust the form also, and, most importantly, to use it. Method acting and the modes of naturalism don't work here.

A few other things to pay attention to:

3

The play is not written in prose. The dialogue is laid out on the page in a poetic form to give the speaker a sense of the musicality, shape and rhythm of each line. Do not try to make the language sound more natural or conversational; if you stick closely to the rhythm of the language it will ground you in your character and have a stronger emotional impact on the audience.

With the exception of George Jones, and his scene with Hattie, there is no subtext in *The Women of Lockerbie*. Every character expresses what they think and feel fully and directly on the line. Not below it.

Keep in mind that every character has a different relationship to the tragedy. This is especially important for the women of Lockerbie. At no point should they get swept into Madeline's energy or get emotional about what has happened to them (Olive's explosion being the only exception). The women's moments in the play are largely contained in the dialogues or odes, which should be in direct contrast in tone and feeling to Madeline's episodes. The Choral dialogues and odes are somewhat matter-of-fact reflections on the event and for the most part are designed to give the audience some distance and breathing room.

The Lockerbie women are above all practical, and not precious, about how to get through this tragedy. "You have to give love," "You have to hate someone" and other such lines should be spoken as if they are simply telling someone how to make a good scone.

A word about emotion in this play: it needs to be carefully controlled. If the actors emote, the audience won't. So, keep the emotion of the play reined in. If you do, then those moments when it does pop out, and there should be very few of them, will be much stronger.

And finally, don't forget the humor. There's a lot of it in the play, just like there was in Lockerbie, Scotland. People are more apt to smile through a tragedy than to frown and humor is one of the ways we get through these things. It's key to helping the audience get through the play, too.

THE WOMEN OF LOCKERBIE was written in 1998 in Copenhagen, Denmark, during a playwriting residency sponsored by New Dramatists. It was further developed through workshops and readings at the Eugene O'Neill National Playwrights Conference, Shenandoah International Playwright's Retreat, Geva Theatre, Oregon Shakespeare Festival, Bay Area Playwrights Festival, Bennington College and New Dramatists. In 2001 it won the silver medal in the Onassis International Playwriting Competition, and was awarded the Kennedy Center Fund for New American Plays award.

THE WOMEN OF LOCKERBIE received its world premiere in New York City on April 6, 2003 in a co-production by the New Group Theatre (Scott Elliott, Artistic Director; Geoffrey Rich, Executive Producer) and Women's Project and Productions (Julia Miles, Artistic Director; Georgia Buchanan, Managing Director) in a special arrangement with Martian Entertainment (Carl White, Tom Smedes and Jamie Cesa). The production was directed by Scott Elliott. The set design was by Derek McLane; the costume design was by Mattie Ullrich; the lighting design was by Jason Lyons; the sound design was by Ken Travis; the dialect coach was Stephen Gabis; and the stage manager was Valerie Peterson. The cast was as follows: Judith Ivey, Larry Pine, Adam Trese, Angela Pietropinto, Kristin Sieh, Jenny Sterlin and Kathleen Doyle.

THE WOMEN OF LOCKERBIE was also produced by the Bloomsburg Theatre Ensemble (Daniel Roth, Ensemble Director; Daniel Cress, Managing Director) in April and May 2005. The production was directed by Laurie McCants. The set design was by Arthur Rotch; the costume design was by Paula Davis-Larson; the lighting design was by A.C. Hickox; the music was by Mary Knysh; the dialect coach was Barry Kur; and the stage manager was Mary Agnes Brown. The cast was as follows: Elizabeth Dowd, James Goode, Leigh Strimbeck, Cassandra Pisieczko, Dodie Rippon-Lovett, Samantha Phillips and Daniel Roth.

CHARACTERS

MADELINE LIVINGSTON, a suburban housewife from New Jersey. Her twenty-year-old son, Adam, was killed in the Pan Am 103 crash over Lockerbie, Scotland.

BILL LIVINGSTON, her husband, father of Adam.

OLIVE ALLISON, an older woman, from Lockerbie. Leader of the laundry project.*

WOMAN 1 and 2, middle-aged women, from Lockerbie.*

HATTIE, a cleaning woman, from Lockerbie.

GEORGE JONES, the American government representative in charge of the warehouse storing the remains from the Pan Am 103 crash.

*Producers are encouraged to increase the size of the women's chorus when possible. If this is done, simply take the lines for Woman 1 and 2 and reassign them among the larger group.

PLACE
The rolling green hills of Lockerbie, Scotland, where Pan Am Flight 103 crashed. There is a stream running between the hills.

TIME
December 21, 1995, the seven-year anniversary of the crash. The night of the winter solstice.

NOTE
*After the crash of Pan Am 103, the women of Lockerbie, Scotland set up a laundry project to wash the 11,000 articles of clothing belonging to the victims that were found in the plane's wreckage. Once the clothes were washed, the women packed and shipped them to the victims' families around the world.

The Women of Lockerbie is a work of fiction and does not purport to be a factual record of real events or real people. Although it is loosely inspired by historical incidents, the names, persons, characters, dates, and settings have been completely fictionalized, as have all of the dramatic situations.

There should be no intermission.

THE WOMEN
OF LOCKERBIE

PROLOGUE

The play begins in darkness. Night has fallen. From offstage, a flashlight sweeps across the hills which are covered with patches of fog.

BILL.
 (Off. Calls out.) Madeline?
 Madeline?!

OLIVE.
 (Off.) Mrs. Livingston?
 (Bill Livingston and Olive Allison enter. Bill carries a woman's coat. Olive carries a flashlight.)

BILL.
 (Calls.) Madeline, sweetheart?
 Where are you?

OLIVE.
 Mrs. Livingston?

BILL.
 Answer me, Maddie! Please!

OLIVE.
 Are you sure she's out here?

BILL.

    Oh yes. I saw her run in this direction.
    (He looks out over the hills.)
    She's roaming the hills again
    looking for our son's remains.
    She's been roaming for two days now
    ever since we got here.
    Morning, noon and night
    that's all she does …
    (Pause.)
    (Calls.) Madeline!
    (Pause.)
    It was all I could do to get her to attend the memorial service.
    And now, she runs out of the church
    before it's over.
    Doesn't even put her coat on.
    She'll catch her death of cold if we don't find her.

OLIVE.

    We'll find her. Don't worry.
    I've lived in Lockerbie my whole life.
    I know these hills like I know myself.
    (Olive sweeps a flashlight over the surrounding hills.)
    (Calls.) Mrs. Livingston?
    Come on, love.
    Come back to us!

BILL.

    It's a helluva night to be out.
    Cold and damp.

OLIVE.

    When the fog clings to the hills like this at night
    it means the morning will be clear.

BILL.

    It's been seven years since he died in the crash.
    Seven long years
    and still
    she can't put aside her grief.

I thought her sorrow would diminish with time.
But it hasn't.
It's as strong today
as it was the day he died.
I don't understand it.
The other families have gone on with their lives.
Why can't she?

OLIVE.
The other families had a body to bury.

BILL.
Yes. The body.
Maybe if she had the body
things would be different.

OLIVE.
With a body
she would have a coffin,
or an urn,
or a gravesite.
A place to put her grief.
But your wife has no such place.
All she has is the sky
where he vanished.
The sky was not meant
to be a burial ground.
It's too big
and when you store your grief there
it runs wild.

BILL.
Yes.
And now that she's here in Lockerbie,
it's running even wilder.
It must be these hills ...
(Pause. He looks out over the hills.)
They've got a
strange
kind of

> *power*
> these hills
> don't they?

OLIVE.
> Yes. They do.

BILL.
> And *beauty* …
> Funny.
> Beauty is the last thing I expected to find in Lockerbie …
> This is the first time we've come here.
> I was afraid to bring her all these years.
> I was afraid it would make her grief even worse.
> And it has.
> I don't know …
> maybe I did the wrong thing
> by bringing her here.
> I just thought that
> *maybe*
> if she came to Lockerbie
> on the anniversary
> to attend the service
> and see the monument
> and meet the other families
> *maybe*
> *then*
> she'll stop weeping.
> She's been weeping for seven years.
> She lies on the living room couch and weeps.
> All day.
> She can't stop.
> Or won't.
> Our friends have given up.
> They don't call or visit anymore.
> Their patience is worn thin.
> *Mine* is worn thin.
> I didn't think it was possible
> for two eyes
> to cry so many tears.

But it is.
I have seen an ocean pour from her eyes.

OLIVE.
There is no greater sorrow than the death of a child.

BILL.
No. There's not.
(Pause.)
He was our only child.
(Pause.)
He was twenty years old.

OLIVE.
Adam Alexander Livingston.

BILL.
You know his name?

OLIVE.
Everyone in Lockerbie
knows the names
of everyone who died.

BILL.
Everyone in Lockerbie is very kind.
You are very kind.
Thank you for coming here with me.
I'm … uh …
I'm at my wit's end here.

OLIVE.
I know you are, love.
We all are.
(Flashlights sweep across the hills.)

FIRST CHORAL DIALOGUE

WOMAN 1.
  (Off.) Olive?

WOMAN 2.
  (Off.) Olive?

WOMAN 1.
  (Off.) Olive?

OLIVE.
  Over here!
  (Olive flashes back with her light.)

WOMAN 2.
  (Off.) Olive, is that you?

OLIVE.
  Aye!
  (Woman 1 and Woman 2 enter, carrying flashlights.)

WOMEN.
  Hello.

BILL.
  Hello.

WOMAN 1.
  You're Mr. Livingston, aren't you?

BILL.
  Yes.

WOMAN 1.
  Are you all right?

BILL.
I'm fine, thank you. It's my wife that's the problem.

WOMAN 2.
Have you found her?

BILL.
No. Not yet.

WOMAN 1.
We saw her run from the church
in the middle of the service

WOMAN 2.
When they lit the candles
and read the names of the dead.

WOMAN 1.
We were worried.

WOMAN 2.
We saw her roaming the hills
this afternoon

WOMAN 1.
Yesterday, too
and the day before.

WOMAN 2.
Can we help?

BILL.
Thank you, but I'm not quite sure what to do.

OLIVE.
Why don't we split up and continue to look for her?

BILL.
This is the place she keeps coming back to.
I think we should stay right here.

OLIVE.
All right, then. That's what we'll do.

WOMAN 1.
Olive, we just got word from Hattie down at the warehouse.

OLIVE.
What's the news?

WOMAN 1.
The mayor came out of the meeting with Mr. Jones.

WOMAN 2.
He didn't succeed.

OLIVE.
Has Mr. Jones announced yet what he's going to do?

WOMAN 1.
No. But he revealed his plans to the mayor.

WOMAN 2.
Olive ...
He's going to burn the clothes.

OLIVE.
Burn the clothes!?

WOMAN 1.
Yes.

WOMAN 2.
Everything on the Shelves of Sorrow
will be incinerated at dawn.

OLIVE.
I was afraid something like this was going to happen.

WOMAN 2.

    (To Bill.) Now that the investigation is over
    and the evidence has been collected against the terrorists,
    they're going to burn the clothing of the victims.

BILL.

    I didn't know there were any.

WOMAN 2.

    There's quite a lot, actually.

WOMAN 1.

    Over 11,000 articles.

OLIVE.

    Why is Mr. Jones going to burn them?

WOMAN 1.

    "Government procedure."

WOMAN 2.

    "Blood and fuel contamination," he told the mayor.

WOMEN 1.

    (To Bill.) The women of Lockerbie have
    petitioned the American authorities in Washington
    to release the clothing to us.

WOMAN 2.

    We want to wash the clothes
    and return them to the victim's families.

BILL.

    Some families may not want them, you know.
    I know that I, for one, wouldn't want them.
    They'd just bring back things that are better left alone.

WOMAN 2.

    Each family can decide for themselves.

WOMAN 1.
Besides, it's something we must do.

WOMAN 2.
Not only for the families, but for ourselves.

WOMAN 1.
We need to give love to those who have suffered.

BILL.
You do? Why?

WOMAN 2.
So evil will not triumph.

BILL.
That's very kind of you.

WOMAN 2.
Not really. We're just doing what we want to.

WOMAN 1.
What we would want others to do for us.

OLIVE.
When evil comes into the world
it is the job of the witness
to turn it to love.

WOMAN 1.
Aye.

OLIVE.
We were the witnesses.
We are simply doing our job.
But

WOMAN 2.
But

WOMAN 1.
But

OLIVE.
Your government has not been very responsive,
I'm sorry to say.

WOMAN 2.
They sent a man from Washington,
Mr. Jones.

WOMAN 1.
George Jones

WOMAN 2.
To shut down the warehouse.
He won't return our phone calls.

WOMAN 1.
He's too busy to bother with us women.

WOMAN 2.
He didn't even attend the memorial service.

WOMAN 1.
He's only been in Lockerbie for two weeks.
He doesn't understand the situation.

WOMAN 2
He didn't see the destruction.

BILL.
What can you do?

WOMAN 2.
(To Olive.) Aye, what's the next step?
Time's running out.
In eight hours, the clothing will be burned.

OLIVE.
Don't worry, Hattie and I worked out a strategy this morning.

WOMAN 2.
(To Bill.) Hattie is the cleaning woman in Mr. Jones' office.

WOMAN 1.
(To Bill.) She's one of us.

OLIVE.
She's going to call Bishop Laing.
He has offered to help.

BILL.
Mrs. Allison …
Please. Don't let me keep you.
It sounds like you are needed in town
with more important matters.

OLIVE.
No. It's best that I work from behind the scenes.

WOMAN 1.
(To Bill.) If Mr. Jones gets wind that Olive is around
he'll call in Scotland Yard!

WOMAN 2.
(To Bill.) The day he arrived in Lockerbie,
she cornered him in the market!

WOMAN 1.
(To Bill.) When he tried to get away,
she grabbed his arm and started to yell!

OLIVE.
I didn't yell.

WOMAN 1.
Olive … dear … you yelled.

OLIVE.
>I spoke … forcefully.
>With great conviction.

WOMAN 1.
>*(To Bill.)* She terrified the poor man!

OLIVE.
>He wouldn't listen to me!

WOMAN 1.
>Olive's going to stay in the background tonight.

WOMAN 2.
>Generals don't belong on the front lines anyway.

OLIVE.
>*(To Bill.)* Besides, I need to be here with you.
>Your wife's struggle with grief
>is the struggle we all share.
>It threatens to tear us apart, too.

BILL.
>It does?

OLIVE.
>*(Pause.)* Aye.

FIRST EPISODE

MADELINE.
>*(Off.)* Adam?

BILL.
>Maddie?

WOMAN 1.
    Is that her?

BILL.
    Yes. Maddie! Over here!

WOMAN 2.
    Where is she?

WOMAN 1.
    There.
    (The women shine their flashlights, catching Madeline as she comes over the hill.)

MADELINE.
    Adam?

WOMAN 1.
    Poor thing.

WOMAN 2.
    Look how she wanders,
    her spirit broken.

WOMAN 1.
    It breaks my heart to see her.

WOMAN 2.
    She is a like a tree
    that's been struck by lightning,

WOMAN 1.
    split down the middle with grief.

MADELINE.
    Adam?

BILL.
    Maddie! Over here!
    (Bill runs to the top of the hill to meet her.)

MADELINE.
    He's here, Bill.
    Adam is here.
    I can feel him.

BILL.
    Maddie, put your coat on.

MADELINE.
    When I walk over these hills
    I can feel him.

BILL.
    Well, good.

MADELINE.
    If only I could find him!
    If only I could find some *part* of him.
    A *bone.*
    The bone
    from his *chin.*
    I would know it if I saw it!
    He had such a
    strong
    firm
    chin …
    What I would give …
    And what I would give to talk to him.
    Even if it was only to say
    "Pick up your socks!"
    And to hear him say, *"Mom!"*
    Remember how he would say that?
    He would rolls his eyes at me and say *"Mommmmm!"*

BILL.
    Yes, I remember.
    I also remember how mad you got
    when he did that.

MADELINE.
I never got mad.

BILL.
You always got mad.
You would shoot him a look
and say, "Don't *Mom!* me!"
(Madeline heads back up the hill.)

BILL.
Where are you going?

MADELINE.
To find him.

BILL.
You won't find him, Maddie.
There is nothing to find.
The bomb went off in the compartment
under his seat.
Everyone in that part of the plane vanished.
You know that.

MADELINE.
There's got to be something of him somewhere!
(Madeline breaks away and runs up the hill.)

BILL.
Maddie, please!

OLIVE.
Mr. Livingston.
You can't reason with grief.
It has no ears to hear you.
Let her walk the hills
and tread her grief into the ground.
Do you think you should go with her?

BILL.
And do what?

OLIVE.
  Walk the hills …
  Tread the ground a little yourself, perhaps?

BILL.
  If I do that, I'll just make matters worse.

OLIVE.
  Alright then.
  We'll stay nearby
  and wait for this
  to run its course.
  (Offstage, a church bell rings.)

WOMAN 1.
  The Candlelight procession has begun.
  They're walking to the town square
  for the all-night vigil.

WOMAN 2.
  Some are going up to Lamb's Hill
  to pray at the stone wall.
  Used to be
  we would celebrate on that wall.
  Remember?

WOMAN 1.
  Aye. The solstice.

WOMAN 2.
  The winter solstice.

WOMAN 1.
  Every December 21st
  we'd go up there and light a bonfire
  then sit all night
  and wait for the return of the sun!

WOMAN 2.
  And when it appeared

we'd pop the cork
and toast the coming of spring!

WOMAN 1.
> Things are different now.

WOMAN 2.
> December 21st is no longer a day of celebration.
> It's a day of mourning.

WOMAN 1.
> A day when we pray for the dead.

BILL.
> Funny.
> The solstice is not something
> we celebrate in New Jersey.
> Don't know why.

OLIVE.
> It's because you're in the middle, love.

BILL.
> The middle?

OLIVE.
> Of the earth.
> Away from the extremes of
> darkness and light.
> *(Madeline appears again at the top of the hill.)*

WOMAN 2.
> *(Whispers.)* Look. Your wife.

WOMAN 1.
> What is she doing?
> *(Madeline walks slowly along the top of the hill. She looks into the sky and speaks silently to herself. The women and Bill watch her from a distance.)*

BILL.
>
> She's talking to herself again.
> She's been doing that a lot lately.
> I come home from work to find her
> sitting at the window
> talking
> to the sky.
> And late at night
> she wanders through the house
> talking to Adam
> as if he were there in the room …

WOMAN 1.
>
> What does she say?

BILL.
>
> She goes over and over
> the moment she heard the news.
> Over and over the moment of his death.
> Just like she's walking these hills now,
> but with words,
> going over and over
> the same ground.

OLIVE.
>
> Grief needs to talk.

BILL.
>
> I've stopped listening.
> I can't take it anymore.

WOMAN 1.
>
> Let us talk to her.
> Maybe she'll listen to us.

WOMAN 2.
>
> And let us listen to her.
> We haven't heard her story before.

WOMAN 1.
> What is old to you is new to us.
> Who knows?
> We might hear something in what she says
> that can help her.

BILL.
> By all means. Go ahead.
> I'll give anything a try.

WOMAN 1.
> *(Calls out.)* Mrs. Livingston?

WOMAN 2.
> *(Calls out.)* Mrs. Livingston, may we talk to you?

MADELINE.
> You want to talk to me?

WOMEN.
> Yes.

MADELINE.
> Want to talk to the crazy lady, huh?

BILL.
> Maddie, please.

WOMAN 1.
> No, that's not why we're here.

MADELINE.
> It's all right if it is.
> It's all right, too, if you think I'm crazy.
> Because I am.

WOMAN 2.
> We don't think you're crazy.

MADELINE.
I'm roaming the hills looking for my son's body.
Only a crazy person would do something like that.

OLIVE.
Or a mother.

MADELINE.
I'm not a mother anymore ...

WOMAN 2.
Mrs. Livingston?

WOMAN 1.
Talk to us. Please.
Tell us your story.

WOMAN 2.
Tell us where you were
and what you were doing
when it happened.

WOMAN 1.
We need to hear it.

WOMAN 2.
And we need to tell our story, too.

OLIVE.
Seven years ago
life as we knew it came to an end
and we are still suffering.

MADELINE.
I was in the kitchen.
I was baking a pie for Adam.
A pumpkin pie, to welcome him home.
The TV was on.
I listen to it when I'm cooking.
It was tuned to a soap opera.

All my Children.
One of the couples was fighting.
The woman was pregnant.
She wanted to get an abortion.
"Don't be a fool!" I say to the woman.
"Have the baby!"
I sprinkle flour on the counter
and roll out the pie dough.
I roll it once in each direction.
Like this ...
(She rolls.)
The way my mother taught me.
And then
Ted Koppel comes on the air.
I know immediately that something is wrong.
You only hear Ted Koppel's voice at night
never in the day.
He said:

BILL.
"We interrupt this program ... "

MADELINE.
I thought,
"Oh dear,
Something awful has happened.
What a shame.
And so close to Christmas."
I grab more flour and sprinkle it.
I roll the crust.
I hear ...

BILL.
"Pan Am 103."

MADELINE.
The pie dough sticks to the rolling pin.

BILL.
"Pan Am 103 was last seen in a fireball over Scotland."

MADELINE.
    I double over.
    I sink onto the kitchen counter.
    My face presses into the pie dough.
    It is cold on my nose and cheek.
    I cannot stand up.
    I grope the counter
    for something to hold on to.
    My arm hits the flour bin.
    It crashes to the floor.
    My feet are covered with flour.
    I reach for the handle
    on the refrigerator.
    I pull myself up.
    And there
    in front of me
    is a note
    held by a magnet
    that says
    "Adam. 7 P.M. JFK. Pan Am 103."
    (Madeline sinks to the ground, overcome with grief.)
    I live in New Jersey!
    I have two cars in the driveway!
    This was not supposed to happen to me!
    (Long pause.)

WOMAN 1.
    You think the worst can't happen.

WOMAN 2.
    You think that it won't.

WOMAN 1.
    But then, one day, it does.

OLIVE.
    The "poor soul" on television
    is suddenly you

WOMAN 1.

>And the faraway disaster
>lies in the flour that falls
>on your kitchen floor.
>*(Olive lifts Madeline back to her feet. She takes a candle from her coat pocket and offers it to Madeline.)*

OLIVE.

>Let's light our candles
>Shall we?
>I brought them from the church.
>We'll keep our vigil here
>together
>in this place where your son died.

MADELINE.

>No!
>*(Madeline breaks away.)*
>Lighting candles will give me no comfort!
>*(Madeline runs to the other side of the hill.)*
>*(Olive turns back to the others.)*

OLIVE.

>I could use the comfort of a candle.

WOMAN 2.

>I could too.
>*(Olive lights her candle. The women light their candles from hers.)*

OLIVE.

>Mr. Livingston?

BILL.

>Please.
>*(Bill takes a candle from his coat pocket. Olive lights it.)*

FIRST CHORAL ODE

"GRIEF"

Olive watches the flame on her candle.

OLIVE.
    Death is a guest whose visit is short
    When it comes to your house
    it never stays

WOMAN 1.
    It just pokes its head in the door
    to drop something off!

WOMAN 2.
    … and is gone.

WOMAN 1.
    But Grief …

OLIVE.
    Grief is a guest who stays too long.
    Its visit turns from days

WOMAN 2.
    into weeks

WOMAN 1.
    into months

OLIVE.
    into years.

WOMAN 2.
    It takes over your house
    and will not leave.

OLIVE.
It wears a dark coat.

WOMAN 1.
It sleeps in your bed all day
and sits in your chair all night.

WOMAN 2.
It rearranges your closets
and cupboards.

WOMAN 1.
It leaves dirty dishes
in the sink.

WOMAN 2.
Wherever you go
it follows.

WOMAN 1.
Whatever you do
it watches.

OLIVE.
It hovers behind you
looking over your shoulder
so you cannot forget
that it's there.

BILL.
Yes …
(They stand in silence, looking at their candles.)

SECOND CHORAL DIALOGUE

WOMAN 2.
    I was driving to the petrol station.

WOMAN 1.
    I was walking the dog.

OLIVE.
    I was baking a pie, like your wife.

WOMAN 2.
    Suddenly the sky turned red.

WOMAN 1.
    The ground shook.

OLIVE.
    The pie fell.

WOMAN 1.
    The tree at the end of the lane burst into flames.

OLIVE.
    I ran to the door.

WOMAN 2.
    I slammed on the brakes.

WOMAN 1.
    I turned and looked.
    My neighbor's rose garden
    was on fire, too.
    Green bushes
    with
    wee
    buds

of fire
where the flowers should have been.

WOMAN 2.
I jumped out of the car.

OLIVE.
I ran out of the house.
There
on top of the hill
was a suitcase.
A red suitcase.
Sitting there
as if someone had
set it down.

WOMAN 1.
People were running from their homes
screaming and crying.

WOMAN 2.
Gordon MacPherson
was kneeling in the street
holding the body of his daughter.
His wife was beside him
pushing her fists
into her eyes.

WOMAN 1.
When I got to my house
the lights were still on
but the roof was gone.
I unlatched the gate
and stepped into the yard.
Someone yelled

OLIVE.
"Don't go in there!"

WOMAN 1.
    But I didn't listen.
    I had to see what had happened.
    I pushed open the door.
    Inside my living room
    was a pile of bodies.
    (Pause.)
    71 bodies still strapped to their seats.

WOMAN 2.
    Suddenly there were helicopters
    and police sirens.
    Down on Lockerbie Lane
    Christmas carols were playing.

OLIVE.
    And up above
    letters
    from mailbags
    fell
    from the clouds.

WOMAN 2.
    They drifted
    to the
    ground
    and covered
    the street
    like snow.
    (Pause.)

WOMAN 1.
    We saw the wreckage.

OLIVE.
    The things they couldn't show on the telly.

WOMAN 2.
    We saw the bodies

WOMAN 1.
    and the body parts

OLIVE.
    strewn
    like *litter*
    along the streets.

WOMAN 2.
    And we saw the faces.

WOMAN 1.
    Oh God, the faces.

OLIVE.
    The faces of the dead.

WOMAN 1.
    It's the faces that haunt me the most.

WOMAN 2.
    Some had been asleep when it happened.
    Their faces were peaceful.

WOMAN 1.
    But others were awake.
    Their faces were frozen
    in horror
    and disbelief.

OLIVE.
    They knew.

WOMAN 2.
    Yes, they knew.

WOMAN 1.
    You could tell they knew what was happening.

SECOND CHORAL ODE

"LOCKERBIE"

The Women are suddenly thunderstruck with the realization that this has happened in Lockerbie.

WOMAN 1.
    We live in Lockerbie.

OLIVE.
    Lockerbie

WOMAN 2.
    Lockerbie Scotland!
    A tidy little town
    with rolling green hills

OLIVE.
    North of the Solway Firth
    in the Dumfries region
    of the Scottish lowlands.

WOMAN 1.
    Where the Annan River
    meets the Kinnel and the Moffat.

OLIVE.
    But not exactly.

WOMAN 1.
    No, not exactly.
    We're off to the side a bit
    off the beaten path

WOMAN 2.
     far away from the troubles of the world.

OLIVE.
     Trouble just doesn't come to Lockerbie Scotland.

WOMAN 2.
     There's nothing for it to do here

WOMAN 1.
     except graze with the sheep
     or take tea in the afternoon.

OLIVE.
     But one day

WOMAN 2.
     Yes, one day
     in an instant

WOMAN 1.
     in a blink of an eye
     a twist of fate
     rained metal on our roofs

OLIVE.
     The fog that clung to our gentle hills
     turned to smoke
     and the gentle rain falling from the sky
     turned to blood.
     (Pause. Bill blows out his candle. Pause. The women watch him.)

WOMAN 1.
     Mr. Livingston?

WOMAN 2.
     Are you alright?

WOMAN 1.
     We've upset you.

BILL.
No. No. I just …
didn't *know*.
That's all.

SECOND EPISODE

*Madeline appears at the top of the hill, talking to herself. The
women and Bill watch her.*

MADELINE.
I never should have let him study in London.
I never should have let him go so far from home.
He was too young.
Much too young to go so far from home.
I should have made him wait for a year.
I should have been more firm.
I should have said no.
I should have just said
"*No, no, no* you cannot go!"
Oh God,
Why didn't I say that…?
(Pause.)
And why did I choose Pan Am over Delta?
There were two boxes on the application form!
Why didn't I
check
the *box*
for *Delta*?
(Pause.)
And I should have let him stay an extra day with his friends!
But I said:
"No, I want you home for Christmas.
I want you home for the party.
You need to hang the Christmas lights for your father,

your father has a bad back and he needs you to help him."
(Pause.)
Oh God …
(Pause.)
And why did I plan the party for Friday?
I should have planned it for Saturday!
If I had planned the party for Saturday
he wouldn't have been on that plane.
He would have come home a day later.
He never would have died.
Yes, if I had planned the party for Saturday,
he never would have died …
(Bill approaches her gently.)

BILL.
Maddie …
we couldn't have the party on Saturday.
Remember?
Saturday was Christmas eve.
We never had the party on Christmas eve.
We always had the party the day before.

MADELINE.
You can have a party on Christmas eve!

BILL.
Yes, but we never did that.

MADELINE.
He could have flown on Delta! —

BILL.
— You didn't like Delta —

MADELINE.
— I could have said,
"*No*, you cannot go to London."
I could have said
"*Yes*, you can come home whenever you want!"

BILL.
    You let him go because you loved him
    And you brought him home because you missed him.
    You did what any mother would do!

MADELINE.
    I should have hung the Christmas lights!

BILL.
    Maddie …

MADELINE.
    I could have gotten up on that ladder myself!

BILL.
    I wouldn't have let you!
    Maddie!
    There was nothing you could have done to stop this.
    This tragedy didn't happen because of you.
    Get ahold of yourself!
    (Madeline turns and heads back to the hills.)
    Maddie!
    Come back, please!
    (Pause.) Maddie?
    (Pause.) Sweetheart?
    (Pause.) Please?
    (Madeline disappears over the top of the hill.)
    Oh God. She's getting even worse.

THIRD CHORAL DIALOGUE

OLIVE.
>Our lives are made of choices.
>Hundreds of little choices
>that determine our fate
>each
>with a consequence
>we cannot see.

WOMAN 1.
>You check the box for Delta
>and your son lives.

WOMAN 2.
>You check the box for Pan Am
>and he dies.

WOMAN 1.
>You walk the dog early one day
>and escape the disaster that falls on your house.

WOMAN 2.
>Or you go to the petrol station
>before you go to the market
>and find yourself standing
>in the middle
>of the wreckage.

WOMAN 1.
>Choices.

WOMAN 2.
>Such *little* choices …

WOMAN 1.
>That create such big results.

OLIVE.
>You duck into a doorway
>to get out of the rain …
>and meet your future husband!

WOMAN 2.
>You take the train
>instead of the bus
>and meet a long lost friend
>you haven't seen in years!

WOMAN 1.
>Sometimes I wonder
>if the choices you make
>are yours at all …

WOMAN 2.
>Or if they're made by something else.
>Something greater, like God.

WOMAN 1.
>Yes.
>Sometimes it seems that these things are fated.

WOMAN 2.
>Fated, yes.
>Meant to happen.

BILL.
>And sometimes it seems that they're not.
>Sometimes it seems they're not meant to happen at all.
>They just do.
>For no reason.

THIRD EPISODE

Madeline storms down the hill.

MADELINE.
> If I ever meet his killers
> I will kill them.
> No.
> I will *more* than kill them.
> I will torment them.
> I will inflict on them
> the measure of pain
> they have brought to me.

BILL.
> Maddie!

MADELINE.
> They should suffer!
> At the very least
> their suffering should equal
> the suffering they've caused!

BILL.
> You can't repay endless suffering.

MADELINE.
> Oh yes you can!
> You know how?
> With *endless pain*!
> That's how!
> And let me tell you,
> Pain
> is a
> *gentle*
> word

to describe what I would do to them
if I ever got the chance!
I would bind their hands and feet
with *wire*!
I would cut them with sharp knives!
I would grind *cigarettes* into their eyes —

BILL.
— Madeline! Stop!
What's got into you?
This is a vigil!
We came here to find peace!

MADELINE.
I want justice!
I won't find *peace* until there is *justice*!

BILL.
That's not justice.
That's revenge.

MADELINE.
Those men killed your son!
They killed 270 people!
They destroyed our lives!

BILL.
I know, but —

MADELINE.
— How can you be so calm!

BILL.
Because rage won't bring him back!
Honey, look, I know you're angry —

MADELINE.
— You're goddamn right, I'm angry!
I didn't deserve this!

BILL.

No you didn't.

None of us did.

MADELINE.

I was a good mother!

And a good wife!

And a good neighbor!

I made cookies for the bake sale!

I gave money to the swim team!

I remembered birthdays!

When someone got sick

I made chicken soup!

I *pitted cherries* and *peeled grapes*

to make your favorite pie!

And this is how I'm repaid?

This is what I get?!

For being thoughtful?

For being a good person?

For leading a good life?

BILL.

Honey, I know.

MADELINE.

No, you don't know!

BILL.

Yes, I do.

It's not fair.

But Maddie.

Life's.

Not.

Fair.

At some point, you have to accept that.

You have to move on.

MADELINE.

Move on?

To *what?*

What *is* there in a day
that's worth moving on to?
Breakfast?
Lunch?
Dinner?
Driving the car?
Talking on the phone?
Playing bridge?
No.
I don't know how anyone could *move on*
after something like this!

BILL.
I moved on.

MADELINE.
You didn't love him as much as I did!

BILL.
Maddie!

MADELINE.
If you did, you wouldn't have gotten over it so fast!

BILL.
Maddie, that's not true!
You know that's not true!

MADELINE.
You cleaned out his room!
You gave away his belongings!

BILL.
I did that to help you!

MADELINE.
You just go on as if nothing has happened!

BILL.
What am I supposed to do?

Stop living?
Spend my days weeping on the couch like you?

MADELINE.
You didn't cry at the funeral!
You didn't cry when you got the news!
You didn't cry at all!

BILL.
How could I, Maddie?
I had to do everything!
I had to do everything
to keep *you* from falling apart!
I had to send the medical records to Scotland.
I had to talk to the friends and neighbors.
I had to talk to the reporters
who stood on our lawn with *cameras*
taking pictures of my grief!
I even had to take his Christmas presents back to the mall
because *you* couldn't stand the sight of them under the tree!
Do you know what that was like?
Can you even imagine it?
Try!
Try to imagine it, just for a moment!
(Madeline runs back to the hills.)
(Bill turns back to the women.)
What do you say to the sales clerk?
What do you say to the 16-year old school girl
standing behind the counter at JC Penney's
who smiles at you and asks
"Why are you returning the sweater, sir?"
Do you tell her?
What do you say?
I just looked at her.
I could tell it was her first job.
Her face was round and soft.
Her hands were still chubby, like a child's.
What do you say to someone so young and innocent?
"This was for my son, but he died?"
"He was blown to bits by a bomb?"

"The plane he was taking home for Christmas … *crashed?*"
What do you say?
What do you say to the pretty young girl
with red and green ribbons in her hair?
I said, "My son … "
(Pause.)
I cannot tell her.
I cannot show my grief,
because to do so would take her innocence from the world.
I just said …
My son doesn't need it anymore."
And then I breathe a sigh of relief
because I think I've gotten through it.
But I haven't.
Oh no!
It doesn't stop there.
She smiles and says
"Would you like to exchange this for something else?"
(Pause.)
Do I want to exchange this for something else?
Oh … yes.
Oh, yes, yes, yes, I do.
Oh, what I would *do*
to turn this in for something else.
But I say,
"No. No, thank you.
Your store doesn't carry what I want or need right now.
Just give me the credit, please."
And then I go to the next store.
To return the Nikes.
And the next store
to return the pajamas.
And the next store
to return the bathrobe and the blue jeans and the bike helmet.
(Pause.)
I go to six stores before the day is through.
I have that same conversation in every single place.
(Pause.)
She's right.
I didn't show my grief.

I couldn't.
I had to keep myself numb just to get through it.
(Bill turns around and looks in the direction of the hills.)
Maddie?
(She doesn't answer.)
(Bill turns around and looks at the women.)
I … I'm sorry …
I …
Oh God.
God.
I don't know what to do.
(He sits on a rock by the stream. Olive gives Bill her candle. Then, she pulls a small book out of her pocket. She opens it and reads. The following Ode is addressed to Bill.)

THIRD CHORAL ODE

"FAITH"

OLIVE.
    (Reads.) The dark forest leads to an open field.
    The dark valley rises to a mountain
    where the sun shines bright.
    Spring follows winter
    and morning, the dark night.

WOMAN 1.
    There's an order in the world.
    An order behind the chaos and the violence.

WOMAN 2.
    And there's a purpose.

WOMAN 1.
    Yes.

WOMAN 2.
>	If the sun never set
>	we would find no beauty in the sunrise.

WOMAN 1.
>	If the night was full of light
>	we would not see the stars.

OLIVE.
>	And if hatred never pierced our hearts
>	we would not know the power of love.

WOMAN 1.
>	These things are given to us for a reason.

OLIVE.
>	Though the reason is never made fully clear.

WOMAN 1.
>	They are given to us so we may learn and grow.

WOMAN 2.
>	And no one is given a burden that they are unable to bear.

WOMAN 1.
>	You have to trust in this.

WOMAN 2.
>	Yes.

WOMAN 1.
>	Trust in the rising sun
>	and in the stars that shine at night.

OLIVE.
>	Trust in the strength of love
>	to overcome the awesome power of hatred.

WOMAN 1.
>	Trust.

WOMAN 2.
    Yes, trust.

OLIVE.
    And believe
    that behind the suffering of the world,
    there is a purpose
    to everything.

FOURTH DIALOGUE

"THE AGON"

Bill responds to the women.

BILL.
    I want to believe that.
    I want nothing more than to believe
    that this has happened for a reason.
    But I can't.
    I just … *can't.*
    To believe that would mean that Adam died
    just so I could learn and grow.
    And that's not true.
    There is no lesson so important
    that it was worth the price of his life.
    To believe that would mean
    that I am at the center of the universe
    and that all things happen for my benefit.
    And they don't.
    The events of the world …
    the horrors …
    just happen.
    And they happen for *no reason.*
    The only thing you can do is accept that

and carry on the best you can.
Just … accept the suffering that comes to you
and find some way to keep going.
Love helps.
Goodness and kindness do too.
But the only reason they are in the world
is not because God gave them to us
but because along the way people discovered
they can make our lives a little easier to bear.
(Pause.)
If there is a God …
and sometimes when I lie in bed at night
I think that there isn't …
But *if* there is,
he is absent from the world
and pays no attention to the needs of men.
(Bill exits.)
(The women watch him disappear over the hill.)

OLIVE.
Oh God …
His words leave me with nothing to hold on to.
(Olive blows out her candle.)

WOMAN 2.
Olive?

WOMAN 1.
Love? Are you alright?

OLIVE.
My faith is hanging by a thread
again
ready to break.
How easily my faith is broken …

WOMAN 1.
Mine too.

WOMAN 2.
    It breaks often, my faith.

WOMAN 1.
    I lose it at night when I'm lying in bed.

OLIVE.
    I lie awake at night too.

WOMAN 1.
    But in the morning
    when the first rays of sun hit my window ...
    it is restored.

WOMAN 2.
    But then the *night* ...

WOMAN 1.
    The night ...

OLIVE.
    The night comes again so quickly, doesn't it?

WOMAN 1.
    Funny.
    The world won't let you keep your faith
    But it won't let you lose it, either.

WOMAN 2.
    No

OLIVE.
    No. *(Slight pause.)* So, what do you do?

WOMAN 1.
    I bake scones.

WOMAN 2.
    I clean the house.
    My house has been spotless for the last seven years.

WOMAN 1.
	And I always bake extra.
	So I can give them to other people.
	(Pause.)

OLIVE.
	I'm going to the warehouse.
	I've got to get the clothes.
	I have to find a way out of this dark valley
	before the night is through.
	(The women blow out their candles and exit.)
	(Silence.)
	(The wind blows softly.)
	(The fog moves slowly across the hills.)

FOURTH EPISODE

George Jones enters, walking quickly.

GEORGE.
	Goddamn it!
	Goddamn those goddamn women!
	(He stops to look behind him.)
	Jesus H. Christ.
	Reporters!
	They called in the *goddamn reporters*!
	(He continues walking again, then stops. He looks out over the hills. He's fearful of this place, and starts to whistle to himself. Then, he checks his watch and exits.)
	(Hattie enters, running. She carries a mop. She shivers from the cold.)

HATTIE.
	Oh Hattie!
	Hattie! You're a fool!

Grabbed your mop but not your coat!
You're going to freeze to death, you are
unless Mr. Jones goes back to the warehouse quickly!
(Hattie stops and looks around.)
Where *is* he?
(Offstage, George whistles to himself again. Hattie jumps when she hears him. She peers offstage in the direction of the whistle.)
(Watching him.) What in the devil is he *doing* out here?
(Pause.) Roaming the hills?
Hmmm …
Maybe he's having a change of heart, he is
and came out here to have a think on it.
(George enters suddenly and sees Hattie.)

GEORGE.
Hattie?
(Hattie runs, trying to hide.)
Hattie!
(George catches her.)
What are you doing out here!
(Pause. Hattie starts to furiously mop the grass.)

HATTIE.
Just cleaning up a bit, Mr. Jones.

GEORGE.
Hattie, you're mopping the *grass*.

HATTIE.
Aye, it's gotten muddy, sir.
From the rains.
I thought if I attacked the problem at the source
I could cut down on the mud
gettin' tracked across your office floor.

GEORGE.
You followed me out here didn't you.

HATTIE.
Why, Mr. Jones, I would never think of doing such a thing!

GEORGE.
You've been spying on me ever since I got here.
Always swishing your mop outside my door
listening to my conversations!

HATTIE.
I swish my mop to clean the mud you track on the floors, sir!

GEORGE.
Do you remember the oath you signed with the American
government?

HATTIE.
Oath, sir?

GEORGE.
The paper you signed. When you took this job.

HATTIE.
Aye, sir, I seem to recall some paper.

GEORGE.
In that paper, there was a provision for spying.
Do you remember that provision, Hattie?

HATTIE.
I'm sorry, sir, but I don't.
You see, I don't read.

GEORGE.
You don't read, huh?

HATTIE.
No. I'm just a cleaning woman, sir.
The only thing I know how to do is mop floors.

GEORGE.
Then what are those *books* you've always got in your pocket?

HATTIE.
Books, sir?

GEORGE.
Yes, *books*.

HATTIE.
Oh, the books.
They're … picture books, full of pictures.

GEORGE.
They're not picture books.
They're *romance* novels.
I see you sneak into the broom closet to read them.
And I hear you *sighing* in there when you do.

HATTIE.
I don't *sigh*, sir!

GEORGE.
You *sigh*.
You *sigh* for the *romance* when you *read* those books.

HATTIE.
No, sir. You're wrong.
I *weep*.
And not for the romance,
but for the *lack* of it.

GEORGE.
Weep, sigh, it's all the same to me.
But you *read*.
And you read that oath before signing it
because I saw you read it!

HATTIE.
No sir! I didn't! I was just moving my eyes!

GEORGE.
Do you know what Washington does to spies, Hattie?

HATTIE.
    No.

GEORGE.
    They put them in jail.

HATTIE.
    Oh.

GEORGE.
    Consider this a warning.
    Stop spying.
    Or I'll have Washington put you in jail.
    (Bill enters from the hills.)

BILL.
    Hello?

GEORGE.
    Hallo?
    (Hattie runs to Bill.)

HATTIE.
    Help!

GEORGE.
    Hattie, get back here!

HATTIE.
    He's going to put me in jail, he is!

GEORGE.
    Hattie!

BILL.
    Who's going to put you in jail?

HATTIE.
    Mr. Jones! He's accusing me of being a spy!

BILL.
>Mr. Jones?
>*The* Mr. Jones?

GEORGE.
>You've heard of me?

BILL.
>Oh yes. The women have told me all about you.

GEORGE.
>Oh no. Are you a reporter?!

BILL.
>No. I'm a tourist.

GEORGE.
>What are you doing here?

BILL.
>I'm … visiting my son. For the holidays.

GEORGE.
>Oh! Well, good. Well, look. Don't listen to what the women say about me. They've got it all wrong.

HATTIE.
>*(To Bill.)* And I say, sir, that the women have got it right. He's a bully, he is.

GEORGE.
>— I am not!

HATTIE.
>— And he ought to be ashamed of himself, picking on an *old woman* like me!

GEORGE.
>I didn't "pick on her!"

HATTIE.

(*To Bill.*) He was picking on me, sir, right before you got here. He chased me over that hill!

GEORGE.

I didn't chase you over the hill!

HATTIE.

Him, a *full-grown man*, chasing *me*, an *old woman* —

GEORGE.

(*To Bill.*) — I didn't chase her! —

HATTIE.

— and then *scaring* me half to death by threatening to put me in *jail*!

GEORGE.

(*Explodes.*) I'm not going to put you in jail!
(*Hattie smiles sweetly.*)

HATTIE.

Alright, then.
I'll be on my way, sir, now that that's settled.
(*Hattie promptly turns to exit.*)

GEORGE.

Wait a minute! Hattie!

HATTIE.

Yes, Mr. Jones?

GEORGE.

Where are you going?

HATTIE.

Back to the warehouse.

GEORGE.
To do what?

HATTIE.
To mop the floor.

GEORGE.
What floor?

HATTIE.
The floor in your office.

GEORGE.
Stay out of my office.

HATTIE.
But there's mud in your office, sir. You didn't wipe your feet —

GEORGE.
— I don't want you going into my office! Do you understand?

HATTIE.
Yes, sir.

GEORGE.
Alright.
(Hattie exits.)
(Calls after her.) You may leave!
(To Bill.) These women are driving me crazy!
Look.
Let me give you a piece of advice
about the Women of Lockerbie.
Don't be fooled by the lace on their collars.
Or the flowers on their teacups.
They're not the sweet little old ladies they appear to be.
They're tigers.
And they're ferocious.
You know what they just did?
They called in the television crews!
The *networks.*

The *American* networks.
They're all down at the warehouse
with their reporters
waiting for a statement from me!
And that's not all.
There are two hundred women with them!
Two hundred women!
With *candles.*
They're trying to create
an international incident, these people.

BILL.
But I thought Lockerbie was already an international incident.

GEORGE.
Lockerbie? Hardly!
The world has forgotten all about Lockerbie.
They forgot about it two weeks after the crash.
But if those women get it back in the news…!
Well, then it will be. And then I'll *never* get out of here!

BILL.
You don't like it here?

GEORGE.
What's to like?
Lockerbie is the Siberia of the State Department!
But.
You have to "do your time" in places like this
before you get the better assignments.
Me, I'd rather be someplace else.
You know, places like …
Kuwait …
Tel Aviv …
The hot spots.
And if I handle this right, I just might get there.

BILL.
Then why are you doing it, if I might ask?

GEORGE.
You mean this business with the clothes?

BILL.
Yes.

GEORGE.
I have orders from Washington.
They want things wrapped up here.
Quickly.
So that's what I'm doing.
Look. This whole affair has gone on long enough.
These people should just get over it.
It's been seven years.
I mean … *move on* for God's sake!
Get a life!
I've tried telling them that,
but of course, they won't listen.
They sent the mayor to see me.
They sent the *bishop*, for God's sake.
Next, they'll probably send in a *mother*!
The mothers are the worst.
They come clutching the baby pictures.
Johnny blowing out the candles on his birthday cake.
Little Timmy smiling with his mouth full of braces.
The mothers will drive you crazy.
There is always a mother
who makes it impossible to do your job.

BILL.
What about the fathers?

GEORGE.
Oh, I have to deal with them too.
But men …
Men are different.
Thank God.
You can always reason with a man.
At least they don't shove those pictures in my face.

(Bill pulls out his wallet and opens it.)
What do you have there?

BILL.
My son's school picture from the sixth grade.
Smiling. With his mouth full of braces.
Look.
(Bill shoves the picture in George's face.)

GEORGE.
(Pause.) Was your son ... uh ... on board?

BILL.
Yes.

GEORGE.
Oh. *(Pause.)* I didn't know ...

BILL.
His body was never found.
He's still out here somewhere.

GEORGE.
(Pause.) I'm ... sorry.
(Pause.) Um. What was his name?

BILL.
Adam. Adam Alexander Livingston.

GEORGE.
Oh, yes. Yes. I, uh, seem to recall it ...

BILL.
And here is a picture when he hit a home run.
In the Little League.
The game was tied and the bases were loaded.

GEORGE.
Yeah?

BILL.
Yeah! He brought them all home.
And here ...
Here is the ticket stub
from the Yankees game I took him to on his last birthday.
I just found this a few minutes ago,
in the pocket of my coat.
Funny.
I haven't worn this coat in years.

GEORGE.
Well, hey.
Hey, hey, hey.
That's great.
So your son was a Yankees fan?
(Bill nods.)
Helluva team, the Yanks.
Helluva owner.
I like George Steinbrenner.
Always have. Always will.
Man knows how to run a team.

BILL.
Yes. Yes he does.
(Pause.)
Mr. Jones.
Do you have children?

GEORGE.
No. No, I don't.
Don't have a wife.
Well, I had one.
Had *two*, actually.
But we never got around to having kids.
You know.

BILL.
Then it might be hard for you to understand
the loss that a parent feels ...

GEORGE.
They say there's nothing worse.

BILL.
They're right. There isn't.
(Pause.) See that hill?

GEORGE.
Yeah.

BILL.
My wife is on the other side of it.

GEORGE.
Right now?

BILL.
Yes.

GEORGE.
Doing what?

BILL.
Looking for my son's remains.

GEORGE.
You're kidding.

BILL.
No.
(George rolls his eyes and whistles.)

GEORGE.
Women. You know?

BILL.
They're not the only ones who feel loss.
Men do too.

GEORGE.
>   Not like that.

BILL.
>   No, not like that.
>   That's the difference, I guess …
>   The women show it and the men don't.
>   And they show it more because we don't.
>   It's not fair, really, now that I think about it.
>   The women have to do their own crying
>   and also, the crying for the men …
>   *(Pause. He reflects for a moment on this realization.)*
>   When Adam died …
>   I cut off the pain.
>   I had to.
>   I couldn't take it.
>   But then …
>   I didn't feel anything else either.
>   Just now
>   when I was walking these hills
>   and found this ticket stub from the Yankees,
>   I felt something.
>   For the first time in years.

GEORGE.
>   You did, huh.

BILL.
>   Yes.
>   *(Slight pause.)*
>   Look at this thing.
>   *(He holds up the ticket stub and looks at it with astonishment.)*
>   It's a piece of paper
>   A *little* piece of paper.
>   Who would have thought
>   that a
>   *little*
>   *piece*
>   *of paper*
>   like this

could have that kind of power?
(Pause.)
George ... those clothes aren't just clothes.
They're not *things*.
They have *life*.
Just like this piece of paper.
Please.
Reconsider your decision.
Release the clothes to the women.

GEORGE.
Look ... I wish I could, *really*, but —

WOMAN 1.
(Off. Calls.) — Mr. Livingston?

WOMAN 2.
(Off. Calls.) — Mr. Livingston?

BILL.
Over here!

GEORGE.
Who's that?

BILL.
The women.

GEORGE.
The *women*?!
Oh shit!
Look, I've got to go, I'll see you later —
— *(George starts to run off.)* —
— *(The women enter.)*

FIFTH EPISODE

OLIVE.
> Mr. Jones.
> *(George stops. He turns around and feigns surprise.)*

GEORGE.
> Oh! Mrs. Allison! Hello!

OLIVE.
> Hello.

GEORGE.
> Mrs. Allison, what are you doing out here? In the middle of the night?

OLIVE.
> I could ask the same of you.

GEORGE.
> Well, yes, I suppose you could.
> *(Pause.)*

OLIVE.
> So...? What are you doing here Mr. Jones?

GEORGE.
> Just getting a little fresh air. And you?

OLIVE.
> I'm looking for you.

GEORGE.
> Oh. Well, look, I'm sorry, but I'm afraid I've got to go —

OLIVE.
> — Mr. Jones —

GEORGE.
— I've got an appointment —

OLIVE.
— In the middle of the night?

GEORGE.
Yes, as a matter of fact.

OLIVE.
It's two o'clock in the morning, Mr. Jones.

GEORGE.
Not in Washington, Mrs. Allison.
So, if you'll excuse me ...

OLIVE.
No, I won't.

GEORGE.
I'm afraid you'll have to.

OLIVE.
I need to talk to you.

GEORGE.
I'm a busy man, Mrs. Allison.

OLIVE.
And I'm a busy woman.

GEORGE.
You certainly are. You've been busy tonight, at any rate.

OLIVE.
I have something very important I need to discuss.

GEORGE.
As far as I'm concerned, there's nothing to discuss.

(George starts to exit — quickly.)

OLIVE.
   Why are you afraid of me?
   (George stops.)

GEORGE.
   I'm *not* afraid of you, Mrs. Allison.

OLIVE.
   Then why are you running away?

GEORGE.
   I'm *not* running away. I'm simply in a rush to get back to the warehouse. I've got a conference call with Washington, if you must know. To discuss the situation here.

OLIVE.
   What situation?

GEORGE.
   You know very well *what* situation.

OLIVE.
   There are many, Mr. Jones.

GEORGE.
   I'm talking about the *circus* going on down at the warehouse. With the reporters. And the women with candles. Very well done, I might add. But it won't work.

OLIVE.
   I didn't create that situation. You did.

GEORGE.
   I did nothing of the sort.

OLIVE.
   Did you think you could burn the clothes and not have anyone notice?

GEORGE.
I didn't think it would turn into an international incident, if that's what you mean.

OLIVE.
If you release the clothes, it won't be.

GEORGE.
I won't be bullied, Mrs. Allison.

OLIVE.
I'm not bullying, Mr. Jones. I'm begging.
(Olive falls to her knees at his feet.)
Please. Release the clothes.
Don't burn them.

GEORGE.
Mrs. Allison ... now, wait ... Don't do that ...

OLIVE.
The families need them. *We* need them.

GEORGE.
Mrs. Allison, here, get up ... *please* ... get up.
(He helps Olive back to her feet.)
Look ...
I would like to release the clothes.
Really. I would.
But I can't.
They're contaminated.

OLIVE.
How can they be contaminated, Mr. Jones? They're *seven* years old.

GEORGE.
They've been sealed in evidence bags ever since the crash. They've never been washed.

OLIVE.
    We'll wash them.

GEORGE.
    I'm sorry, but I can't let you do that.

OLIVE.
    Why not?

GEORGE.
    Because. Whenever there is an incident at altitude —

OLIVE.
    — I'm sorry ... a ... *what?*

GEORGE.
    An incident at altitude.

BILL.
    A plane crash.

GEORGE.
    ... Right.
    Involving an American aircraft
    outside of the United States,
    the State Department has certain policies.
    Certain *procedures.*
    For disposal and containment.
    And releasing the clothing of the victims to civilians
    is not one of them.

OLIVE.
    Make an exception.

GEORGE.
    I can't make an exception.

OLIVE.
    Mr. Jones, you can always make an exception.

HATTIE.
That's right! And the State Department allows for exceptions too!
It says so right here in their regulations!
(Hattie pulls a piece of paper out of her pocket.)

GEORGE.
I thought you said you couldn't read, Hattie!

HATTIE.
I lied.

GEORGE.
Look, the regulations don't apply here.
This is a foreign policy matter.
Every action here must be *weighed*
according to a whole different set of criteria.
And *justified*.

WOMAN 2.
Well, that's no problem, Mr. Jones. We've got the perfect justification.

GEORGE.
Oh you do, huh.

WOMAN 1.
Yes, we do.

GEORGE.
And what's that.

THE WOMEN.
Love!

GEORGE.
Ladies. I can't use *love* as a justification.

OLIVE.
Why not.

GEORGE.

Because *love* is not a good enough reason!

OLIVE.

There is *no better reason* than love!

GEORGE.

Tell that to my boss.

OLIVE.

I will. Where is he?

GEORGE.

Look. Excuse me for being blunt.
But you're are getting too caught up in your emotions
to see the big picture.
Try to consider my perspective for a moment.
I have a responsibility here.
A responsibility to reduce the trauma
that has already come to this community
And to look out for its welfare.
For *your* welfare.

OLIVE.

The Scottish people are quite capable
of looking out for our own welfare, Mr. Jones.
We don't need you or the American government
to do that for us.

HATTIE.

This is why no one likes Americans, sir.
You think you know what's best for everyone.

WOMAN 2.

Aye. This is *Scotland!*

WOMAN 1.

The American government should have *no say*
about what happens over here!

GEORGE.

The bomb was an attack on the American government,
ladies.

We have *everything* to say about it.

Look.

You have no idea what you're asking for.

Let me spell it out for you.

The clothes are contaminated.

They're covered in *blood.*

A lot of blood.

Blood from *270 people.*

And that's not all.

There are guts on those clothes.

Guts.

Do you understand?

The clothes are not a pretty sight.

I can't let you see them!

I can't let anyone see them!

I mean, ladies, *trust* me

it will make you *sick* just to look at them!

They made *me* sick.

OLIVE.

Mr. Jones you seem to forget

that we were here when the crash occured.

The things we have seen are worse than those clothes.

WOMAN 2.

The things we have *touched* are worse, too.

Mr. Jones …

I picked up *body parts.*

WOMAN 1.

I did too.

I found a woman's hand

and a child's leg

in my garden.

I picked them up with my own two hands

and carried them down to the morgue.

(Pause.)

GEORGE.
You did?

WOMAN 1.
Yes.

HATTIE.
Everyone did.
(Pause.)

GEORGE.
You are very strong.
I wouldn't have been able to do that.

OLIVE.
Sure you would have.
You find the strength to do what you have to, Mr. Jones.

GEORGE.
I still have the families to think about.
They haven't seen what you've seen.
The sight of the clothes
— washed, or unwashed —
could be devastating.

BILL.
Why don't you let the families decide that for themselves.

GEORGE.
I don't want to open old wounds.

OLIVE.
But you won't, Mr. Jones. You'll heal them.

GEORGE.
Well, that's where you and I disagree.
If you ask me, the best way to heal a wound
is to leave it alone.
And that's what I intend to do.

I'm sorry.
I know that's not what you want to hear.
But that's the way it is.
(George begins to exit.)

OLIVE.
Mr. Jones, wait!

GEORGE.
That's my decision.
I'm not going to discuss it any further.
Hattie?

HATTIE.
Sir?

GEORGE.
If you want to keep your job, I expect to see you back at the
warehouse.

HATTIE.
Yes, sir.
(George exits.)

OLIVE.
But — Mr. Jones!

WOMAN 2.
Let him go, Olive.

OLIVE.
Mr. Jones!

WOMAN 1.
His mind is made up, love. You can't change it.

OLIVE.
But — he —
Oh!
Men like that!

WOMAN 1.
Steady yourself, love.

WOMAN 2.
Getting upset won't do any good.

OLIVE.
We can't let him do that!

WOMAN 1.
You can't stop him, love.

WOMAN 2.
You've done everything you possibly could.

HATTIE.
Not *everything*.

WOMAN 1.
What do you mean, Hattie?

HATTIE.
We can just take them.

WOMAN 1.
Take them?

WOMAN 2.
You mean, the *clothes*?

HATTIE.
Yes.

WOMAN 1.
But …

WOMAN 2.
How do we do that?

HATTIE.
I'll let you in through the back entrance. Where there isn't a
guard.

WOMAN 1.
And then what?

HATTIE.
We take the clothes and bring them back here!

WOMAN 1.
But Hattie! There are 11,000 pieces of clothing!

WOMAN 2.
We can't carry 11,000 pieces of clothing!

HATTIE.
— Of course we can!

WOMAN 2.
How!?

HATTIE.
Because ... there will be 200 of us carrying them!
I'm going to open the front gates.
and let the women inside, too.
In front of the reporters and the *cameras* ...

WOMAN 1.
Hattie, you'll be arrested.

HATTIE.
Yes. I know.
We all will.
But the clothing won't be burned.
Not if the telly is showing pictures of
200 women going off to jail
for wanting to do the laundry.

OLIVE.
You're right!
Come on, let's go.

HATTIE.
No. You stay here.

OLIVE.
But —

HATTIE.
— We need you out here.
To talk to the reporters!

MADELINE.
— *(Off. Calls out.)* Adam?

HATTIE.
We've got to go.

OLIVE.
Hattie, wait —

HATTIE.
— We don't have much time. Come on!
(Hattie and the women exit quickly.)

BILL.
I hope this works.

OLIVE.
I do too …

SIXTH EPISODE

MADELINE.
> *(Off. Calls out.)* — Adam?
> *(Madeline appears at the top of the hill. She watches the women exiting in the distance. She doesn't see Olive and Bill.)*
> They're gone.
> Gone.
> They lit their candles and went back to town.
> They have forgotten you, Adam.
> Just like the world has forgotten.
> But I remember.
> And these hills remember too.
> Look how black they are …
> Even the moon won't shed its light on them.
> *(Madeline goes to the stream. She stands very still, looking at the water.)*
> The water's black, too.
> How quickly you passed …
> One moment here.
> *(Madeline steps to the other side of the stream.)*
> The next moment there.
> *(Madeline steps back to the other side of the stream.)*
> Here.
> *(Then she steps across it again.)*
> There.
> *(She steps back and forth across the stream several times in silence.)*

BILL.
> *What* is she doing?

OLIVE.
> Jumping back and forth across the stream …
> *(Madeline crosses the stream.)*

MADELINE.
> Living.

(Madeline crosses the stream.)
Dead.
(Madeline crosses the stream.)
Living.
(Madeline crosses the stream.)
Dead.
(She stands very still and doesn't cross the stream again.)
Dead.
(Pause.)
Dead, dead, dead.
(Pause.)
What
is it like
to be dead?
What
was it like
when you crossed the line
and passed to the other side?
Were you drinking a coke?
Eating your peanuts?
Taking a nap?
Or were you talking…?
Having a nice conversation
with the woman right beside you?
Mrs. Corcoran.
Yes, Doris Corcoran, her name was.
She was a teacher
from Syracuse University.
What were you saying to her?
Were you talking about London?
Christmas?
College?
Changing your major to math?
And what …
did you
do
the moment it happened…?
Did you grab Mrs. Corcoran's hand?
Hold on to the arm rests?
Close your eyes and pray?

Or did it happen too fast for any of that?
And what happened next?
Adam …
What
happened
next?
What did you do?
Where did you go?
You must have gone *somewhere*
You have to be *someplace* …
(Madeline turns to go back to the hills.)

BILL.
Maddie …

MADELINE.
I thought you were gone.

BILL.
No, I'm still here.

MADELINE.
Leave me alone.
(Bill fishes the Yankee ticket out of his pocket.)

BILL.
I found something of Adam's …

MADELINE.
You did?

BILL.
Yes.

MADELINE.
What?

BILL.
This.
Look.

It's the ticket stub from the Yankees game
I took him to on his birthday.
(Madeline comes back to him. She takes the ticket.)

MADELINE.
Where did you find this?

BILL.
In the pocket of this old coat.

MADELINE.
Where's the other ticket?
There should be two.
Not just one.

BILL.
Well, I only found this one, Maddie —

MADELINE.
— If it was in your pocket, it's not Adam's.
It's *yours.*

BILL.
Yes, but —

MADELINE.
— I don't want anything of yours!
I only want something of Adam's!
(She throws the ticket on the ground and walks away. Bill grabs her.)

BILL.
God you are stubborn!

MADELINE.
Let go of me!

BILL.
Why do you hold on to your grief so hard!

MADELINE.
It's the only thing I have left to hold on to!

BILL.
You have *me*!
Hold on to *me*!

MADELINE.
I don't want you!
(She pushes him away.)

OLIVE.
Don't turn your hatred towards your husband, Mrs. Livingston.

MADELINE.
You stay out of this!

OLIVE.
He's all you've got left.

MADELINE.
Who are you anyway?

OLIVE.
I'm only trying to help.

MADELINE.
I don't want your help!

OLIVE.
You need help —

MADELINE.
— You don't know what I need!

OLIVE.
— Yes, I do —

MADELINE.
— Go away —

OLIVE.
    — No —

MADELINE.
    — this has nothing to do with you! —

OLIVE.
    — It has everything to do with me —

MADELINE.
    — You have no idea what I've been through! —

OLIVE.
    — Yes I do! —

MADELINE.
    — You didn't lose a son in the crash! —

OLIVE.
    — No, I lost a daughter and a *husband*!
Your son's plane fell on my farm
and killed my family!
My daughter is dead!
My husband is dead!
A plane full of *Americans*
killed everyone I love!
I hate Americans!
You started this whole thing, you know!
You bombed that passenger jet from Iran!
You shot down a plane full of innocent people!
Lockerbie was the revenge for that!
You probably don't even know about it!
You were too busy baking your pies
and driving your big cars
and living in your big houses
to pay any attention!
You Americans!
A bunch of cowboys
galloping through the skies

dropping bombs!
I hate you!
I hate you for this!
(Olive charges Madeline and starts to hit her. Women 1 and 2 enter.)

WOMAN 1.
    Olive!

WOMAN 2.
    Olive!

WOMAN 1.
    Olive, stop!

WOMAN 2.
    Olive, what are you doing?!

WOMAN 1.
    Olive!
    (Olive and Madeline fall to the ground.)

OLIVE.
    Oh ...

WOMAN 2.
    Olive ...

OLIVE.
    Oh ... my ...

WOMAN 1.
    Come on, love.
    Get up.
    Love?
    (Olive and Madeline lie in a heap on the ground.)

OLIVE.
    I ...
    Oh my ...
    I ...

Oh God.
I need to wash.
Where are the clothes?
I need to wash.

WOMAN 1.
    We don't have the clothes Olive.

OLIVE.
    … you don't?

WOMAN 1.
    No.

MADELINE.
    What clothes?

WOMAN 2.
    From the crash.

MADELINE.
    There are *clothes*?

WOMAN 2.
    Yes. But we don't have them.

WOMAN 1.
    We were inside the warehouse, Olive.

WOMAN 2.
    We got all the way to the Shelves of Sorrow.

WOMAN 1.
    But we were caught.

WOMAN 2.
    They let us go
    but Hattie's been detained.

WOMAN 1.
    And that's not all …

WOMAN 2.
    The fuel trucks have arrived.

OLIVE.
    … fuel trucks?

WOMAN 2.
    Yes. They're starting the incineration now.

WOMAN 1.
    They won't wait until morning.

WOMAN 2.
    They're burning the clothes tonight.
    (Madeline gets up.)

WOMAN 1.
    Mrs. Livingston?
    (Madeline doesn't answer. She starts to exit in the direction of the warehouse.)

WOMAN 2.
    Mrs. Livingston, where are you going?
    (Madeline exits.)
    (Olive gets up off the ground. She starts to exit in the direction of the warehouse.)

WOMAN 1.
    Olive!

WOMAN 2.
    Olive, wait! We're coming with you.

OLIVE.
    No.

WOMAN 2.
But Olive …

OLIVE.
No.
(Olive exits. Bill picks up the ticket stub lying on the ground. He looks at it for a moment, then puts it in his pocket.)

WOMAN 1.
Mr. Livingston, what's going on?

WOMAN 2.
What happened?
(Bill starts to leave.)
Mr. Livingston? Where are you going?

BILL.
To get my things at the hotel.
I'm leaving.

WOMAN 2.
But why?

WOMAN 1.
Your wife will need you when she gets back.

BILL.
No she won't.
My wife doesn't want me anymore.
She doesn't love me anymore either.
In fact, she hates me.
And what's worse …
I hate her too.

WOMAN 1.
Of course you do. That's only natural.

BILL.
Natural? To hate my wife?

WOMAN 2.
    You have to hate someone.

WOMAN 1.
    Mr. Livingston …
    Hatred is love that's been injured.
    If you have hatred in your heart
    it means you have love in it also.

WOMAN 2.
    Your hatred will turn again to love.
    And your wife's will too, when she heals.

BILL.
    But she won't heal.
    She refuses to.

WOMAN 2.
    She will. You just have to wait.

BILL.
    I've been waiting for seven years!

WOMAN 1.
    Maybe waiting's not enough, love.
    Maybe you need to do something else.

BILL.
    Like what?

WOMAN 1.
    Like … grieving.
    You didn't let yourself grieve …
    (Pause.)

WOMAN 2.
    If you let yourself grieve
    maybe your wife will let herself heal …
    (Pause.)
    Here. Sit down.

WOMAN 1.
    Yes. Sit here with us. Please.

WOMAN 2.
    Don't go back to the hotel.
    Your wife may not need you right now,
    but we do.

BILL.
    You do?

WOMAN 1.
    Yes. We are frightened.

BILL.
    I guess I'm a little frightened too …
    (Pause.)
    Alright.
    (They sit on rocks. They sit in silence for a moment.)

WOMAN 1.
    I'm shaking.

WOMAN 2.
    I'm shaking too.

WOMAN 1.
    Oh God … the things we have seen tonight.

BILL.
    Yes.

WOMAN 2.
    Yes.
    It was our first time in the warehouse.

WOMAN 1.
    Our first time in the Shelves of Sorrow.

WOMAN 2.
It was like living once again through the horror.

WOMAN 1.
We walked through the wreckage,
past the metal

WOMAN 2.
mountains of metal
stacked higher than the hills!

WOMAN 1.
I felt so small walking past them ...

WOMAN 2.
When we entered the shelves
with items from the cabin
I cried.

WOMAN 1.
I did too
when I saw the seat cushions
covered with blood
and the pillows and the blankets

WOMAN 2.
and the trays from the seat backs
piled
neatly
in a stack.

WOMAN 1.
How *neatly* everything is stacked
on the Shelves of Sorrow.

WOMAN 2.
Aye.
So ... orderly.
And arranged.

WOMAN 1.
    Everything

WOMAN 2.
    marked

WOMAN 1.
    with a number.

HATTIE.
    (Off. Calls out.) Mr. Livingston?

WOMAN 1.
    Hattie?

WOMAN 2.
    Hattie?

HATTIE.
    (Off. Calls out.) Mr. Livingston!
    (Hattie enters running.)
    Your wife! Your wife!

WOMAN 1.
    What happened, Hattie?

WOMAN 2.
    Tell us what happened!
    (Hattie tries to catch her breath.)

HATTIE.
    When she arrived…!
    At the warehouse…!
    Olive was with her…!
    When they saw the fuel trucks
    lined up at the warehouse
    they fell to their knees
    and started to wail.
    The crowd of women
    fell to their knees, too

and wailed with them,
two hundred women
kneeling at the gate and wailing
until the night air was filled
with the cries of the Women of Lockerbie.
And then…!
The fuel trucks *stopped* their engines!
The door to the warehouse opened.
Mr. Jones stepped outside.
He ordered the fuel trucks to begin.
But the drivers got out of their trucks!
Mr. Jones marched over to the drivers
and ordered them again.
But they folded their arms
and refused to move!
And then … the cameras started flashing!
The reporters called out his name!
The women wailed even louder!
And then …
suddenly!
Mr. Jones
turned
and walked to the gate!
When he saw Olive and your wife
kneeling on the ground
he just stood there
and looked at them
for a long, long time.
And then …
he reached in his pocket,
pulled out a *key*
and unlocked the gate!
He lifted the two women from the ground
and threw open the gates for the others to enter.
And then, with television cameras flashing all around him
he led all 200 women into the warehouse!
When they got to the Shelves of Sorrow,
Your wife searched
for a bag with your son's name.
But there was none.

She searched through the boxes.
Nothing.
When she got to the shelf marked "Unidentified Remains"
your wife ripped open the bags
the bags full of bloody scraps
looking for a scrap of your son
and still, she couldn't find one.
And then, she went wild.
She stormed through the warehouse
pulling items from the shelves.
She knocked down a stack of dinner trays
and the passenger seats.
She threw down the overhead bins too
and a television monitor.
She punched through the television monitor!
And then, she fell to her knees
and started to scratch herself.
She scratched her arms
and her chest
and her breasts
until they were bleeding ...

SEVENTH EPISODE

Madeline enters walking slowly. Her chest, arms and neck are covered with blood from scratching herself. She stops and stands very still, looking out over the hills.

MADELINE.
There is nothing of Adam's
on the Shelves of Sorrow ... .
(Pause.)
The day he was born
his feet were as long as my little finger.
Do you remember Bill?
Remember how little they were?

I spent *hours* looking at his toes ...
so
tiny ...
And then
suddenly!
he was *sixteen*!
One morning I went to his room to wake him for school.
His foot was sticking out from the covers.
It was big.
And there was hair
on his big toe ...
Three
little
hairs
that announced
his arrival
into manhood.
(Olive enters with a bag of clothing.)

WOMAN 1.
Olive ...

WOMAN 2.
The clothes...?

OLIVE.
Yes. We've got the clothes.
All this time
I've been trying to turn their hatred into love.
But the hatred I needed to turn
was my own.

HATTIE.
I'm full of hate, too.

OLIVE.
Are you, love?

HATTIE.
Aye. I hate the men who did this.

WOMAN 1.
    I hate them too!

WOMAN 2.
    We all do!

OLIVE.
    Well, then.
    Evil has triumphed here after all.
    Hasn't it?
    Mrs. Livingston …
    You're bleeding.

WOMAN 2.
    Yes. She's hurt herself.

OLIVE.
    (Gently.) You need to wash, love.

WOMAN 2.
    (Gently.) Yes. Come to the stream, Mrs. Livingston.

WOMAN 1.
    (Gently.) Let us wash you.

MADELINE.
    No.
    (Madeline opens her blouse to expose her chest, covered with scratches.)
    This
    is his
    gravestone.
    I want everyone to see it.
    My body will be a monument
    to his memory.
    I want everyone who looks at me
    to see what happened to my son!

OLIVE.
    (Gently.) Your son deserves a better monument than that.

Scratch marks and sorrow are not
a fitting way to remember him.
Just as a heart full of hatred is not worthy
of my husband and daughter.
(Olive sets down the bag of clothing.)
We are going to wash the clothes, Mrs. Livingston.
To make our hearts pure again.
That will be our monument to those who died here.
Will you join us?
(Madeline doesn't answer.)
(George Jones enters carrying a suitcase.)

GEORGE.
This is your son's.
I found it with the luggage.
His clothes are still inside,
just as he packed them.
(George sets it down in front of Bill.)
I thought you should have this.
(Madeline crosses to Bill and takes the suitcase.)
(Madeline starts to open it, then stops.)
(She looks over at Bill.)

MADELINE.
Do you want to open it, Bill?

BILL.
Yes, Maddie. I think I need to do that.
(She sets the suitcase down gently in front of him.)
(Pause. Bill slowly opens the suitcase.)
Look.
The T-shirt he always slept in …
(Madeline takes out the T-shirt.)

MADELINE.
Oh, look at this thing!
Full of stains and holes.
I told him not to take this to London!
But I guess he snuck it into his suitcase …
(Madeline looks at the T-shirt.)

Look. Inside.
(They look inside the shirt.)

BILL.
His name.
You always put his name on everything.

MADELINE.
He got so mad at me when I did that!
(Bill takes another shirt out of the suitcase.)

BILL.
Maddie, look.
A T-shirt he got in London …
(Pause.)
He put his name inside it too.
(Bill weeps openly for the first time.)
(Madeline comforts him.)

GEORGE.
So …
if you'll excuse me …
I've got to go.
There's a press conference.
I've got to make a statement
and somehow salvage this situation.
(George starts to leave. Olive stops him.)

OLIVE.
Mr. Jones?

GEORGE.
Yes, Mrs. Allison?

OLIVE.
What are you going to say?
In your statement?

GEORGE.
I don't know yet.

But it won't be about *love*,
I can tell you that.

OLIVE.
Why don't you say something about hatred, then?

GEORGE.
Hatred?

OLIVE.
Yes.

GEORGE.
Like what?

OLIVE.
Like ... "Hatred will not have the last word in Lockerbie."

GEORGE.
"Hatred will not have the last word in Lockerbie."
That might work.
It would certainly make a good headline.

OLIVE.
Yes, it would.
Especially since it's true.

GEORGE.
Well, yes, yes, I suppose it is.
(Pause. George thinks.)
Alright, Mrs. Allison.
That's what I'll say.
Thank you.

OLIVE.
Thank you.
(George reaches out and gives Bill an awkward pat on the shoulder.)

GEORGE.
Ladies.

(George Jones exits.)
(Olive kneels by the bag of clothing. The women gather around her.)

OLIVE.
    Let the washing begin.
    (Olive slowly opens the bag.)
    (The women look inside, but stop. They are overcome by the sight of the clothes.)
    (Olive closes the bag.)
    I … I don't know if I'm strong enough to do this…!

FOURTH CHORAL ODE

"WASHING"

Madeline goes to Olive. She gently takes the bag and opens it for her. When Olive doesn't reach inside, Madeline takes out a piece of clothing and hands it to her. Then, she takes out a piece for each of the women. She takes one for herself, then leads Olive and the women to the stream.

They kneel.
Madeline is the first to wash. The others follow.
They wash.
They wash.
They wash in silence for a long time.
The stage slowly floods with light.
It is dawn.
The hills, which were black in the night turn green with the morning light.

End of Play

PROPERTY LIST

Candles
Woman's coat (BILL)
Flashlight (OLIVE)
Small book (OLIVE)
Mop (HATTIE)
Wallet (BILL)
Photo (BILL)
Yankees ticket stub (BILL)
Paper with regulations (HATTIE)
Bag of clothing (OLIVE)
Suitcase (GEORGE JONES)
2 T-shirts (MADELINE, BILL)

SOUND EFFECTS

Church bells

NOTES
(Use this space to make notes for your production)

NOTES
(Use this space to make notes for your production)

NOTES
(Use this space to make notes for your production)